MANIFESTO
For a Global Civilization
By
Matthew Fox, Theologian
&
Brian Swimme, Physicist

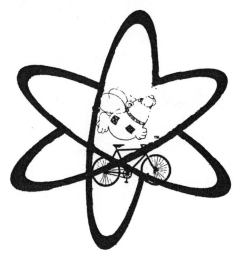

Bear & Company
Santa Fe, New Mexico

Bear & Company, Inc.
P.O. Drawer 2860
Santa Fe, NM 87504

Printed in the United States by George Banta & Company

Second Printing

TABLE OF CONTENTS

5   NEWS FROM CREATION:
    A PROLOGUE

9   I. THREE BOILING POINTS IN
    WESTERN CULTURE

21 II. COSMOGENESIS, CREATIVITY,
    COMPASSION: THE ROOTS OF
    THE GLOBAL CIVILIZATION

33 III. REVISIONING SCIENCE, RELIGION,
    AND THE ART OF LIVING

51 EPILOGUE

NEWS
FROM
CREATION:
A PROLOGUE

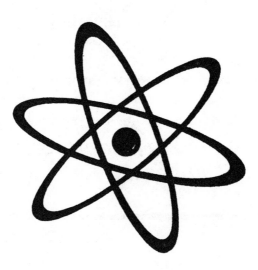

Our era lures us to create the first global civilization on Earth. We are that generation that begins the creative transformation of the whole world into a single community out of the diverse peoples of the planet. The people of the seventeenth century re-created the civilization of the West into the scientific-technological era that we are leaving. The people in the thirteenth century of the Christian era recreated the West into the Christian Middle Ages. Previous to these, people were moved to create what would become the Western roots in the axial philosophic civilization of the Greeks and the axial religious civilization of the Hebrews. So too, we as a people find ourselves in a unique moment for creating this transformation leading to the first global civilization. However monumental were the creations of the scientific civilization, or the Christian Middle Ages, or the Greek or Hebrew civilizations, none of these achievements can be used as a standard with which to measure the magnitude of the present transformation. Indeed, only by picturing the very beginning of civilization when the people of Sumer in 3500 B.C. moved out of the tribal modality of being and created the first civilization on Earth can we find a movement in history of an immensity analogous with our own.

A civilization is a community of beings united in a common aim of creating the beautiful.

A civilization is a community of beings united in a common aim of creating the beautiful. In this sense, the global civilization is initiated with the expression of its overarching vision, for this is what gathers a community of humans into the task of creating a civilization. Though cultural chaos dominates the global situation of our time, the vision of what is to come can gather us into the work of creation even in the midst of collapse and confusion. The chaotic fragmentation that surrounds the globe represents the confusion that accompanies every great birthing hour. The world quails with the fear of labor, and it is the task of our generation to act as midwife to this great birthing, to assist in the cosmological movement itself by creating those forms of life and being that will usher in the era of the global civilization.

The world quails with the fear of labor, and it is the task of our generation to act as midwife to this great birthing.

This manifesto is an articulation of those fundamental forms of thought that are sure to characterize the global civilization in a broad fashion. It is, in intellectual form, the vision of the beautiful that is not yet actuality but that lures us as a community into the creation of ourselves and our world. As such, this manifesto is an invitation to an adventure in creating a Global Civilization which will usher in a new era in the divinization of the cosmos.

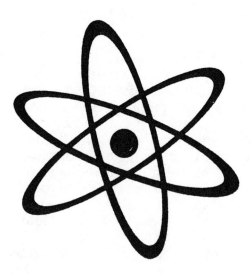

I.
THREE
BOILING
POINTS
in
WESTERN
CULTURE

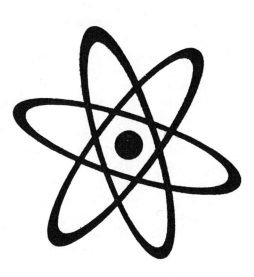

We create ourselves and our world out of the context of our present culture. In the west, the news of the twentieth century is that our culture is boiling. We are boiling over into the creation of the global civilization, a boiling that will in time permeate all levels of being in all sectors of the culture. We here examine this metamorphosis by focusing on three boiling points taken from significant movements in twentieth century physics, mathematics and religion respectively. They are as follows: the indivisibility of the quantum of action; the incompleteness of the theoretical system; and the inseparability of divinity-world in the creation-centered spiritual tradition.

Indivisibility of the Quantum Action

For three centuries the West has labored under a mechanical understanding of the world. We have understood the universe as a place where inert particles interacting with one another form the basis of the world itself. Because science was structured on the assumption that the world could be analyzed in terms of these relatively autonomous parts or particles, and because science showed itself as tremendously powerful, the West recreated all its forms of life in response to the fundamental assumptions of science. Economics, religion, social sciences, medicine, politics and governments, every aspect of culture eventually reflected the underlying mechanical understanding of the world that grounded science. The West fragmented into all the micro-specialties that splinter our universities even today. With a world view based on a parts-mentality, we humans created a parts culture, a fragmented and centerless attempt at the fullness of civilization.

But through the work of Albert Einstein, Max Planck, Werner Heisenberg, Erwin Schroedinger, Niels Bohr, and Paul Dirac we have come to understand that the world is, at its most primal level, an undivided whole. We have

---

With a world view based on a parts-mentality, we humans created a parts culture, a fragmented and centerless attempt at the fullness of civilization.

---

uncovered the inadequacy of the parts-cosmology, have broken through this limited and limiting perspective to an understanding of the wholeness that grounds all of reality. The work of these theoretical physicists and many more besides has shattered the structures of our world view, and created the foundations of another world radically distinct from the past one. Whereas it was the core of classical scientific theory to speak of particles-in-interaction as the beginning point in any discussion of the world, this is now understood as at best a high level abstraction. Rather, twentieth century quantum physics reveals the undivided wholeness of the experimental situation as the ground for scientific understanding. The creative achievements of theoretical physics in our century establish one undivided world as the starting point for scientific analysis.

The fundamental symbol for the classical scientific world view was the billiard table with the billiard balls glancing off one another. The fundamental symbol for the world

11

view that has emerged from twentieth century theoretical physics is that of the musical symphony. Though a careful understanding of quantum physics demands an understanding of its mathematics, the symbol that best grasps the new world view implicit in the mathematics is the

The fundamental symbol for the classical scientific world view was the billiard table with the billiard balls glancing off one another.

symphony, the world itself as symphony. For with the symphony, we are compelled to begin with the wholeness of the music altogether before we attempt any analysis or discussion of the music. Indeed, to speak of the leitmotif of the second movement of Beethoven's ninth as if this leitmotif could be discussed in its entirety, in its fullness, and in all its meaning without considering the whole from which it has been abstracted is an absurdity. In an analogous manner, to attempt to speak of the electron in an experiment as if this electron could be discussed and understood in its full meaning without consideration of the whole experimental situation is without scientific validation. The experimental situation is an indivisible

The fundamental symbol for the world view that has emerged from twentieth century theoretical physics is that of the musical symphony.

whole, and to speak of an electron is to speak of an aspect of the wholeness, an aspect that has its meaning only in relationship to this wholeness.

The past age of modernity was grounded on the fundamental assumption that the world was based on particles that interacted externally; the emerging global civilization is grounded on the understanding that the world is an undivided whole. Whereas the machine was the primary symbol for the world in the previous age, in the emerging age the primary symbol for the world is music. This boiling point is not only boiling in theoretical physics; or in the basic sciences; or in the general culture. This boiling point is boiling in the heart of the human

---

The past age of modernity was grounded on the fundamental assumption that the world was based on particles that interacted externally; the emerging global civilization is grounded on the understanding that the world is an undivided whole.

---

being who is immersed in creating the radically new forms of life of the global civilization of compassion. To begin with the assumption that the world is music is to enter the way of re-creating the meaning of human being and thereby the world.

The Incompleteness of the Theoretical System

The second Boiling Point concerns the mathematical proof of the essential incompleteness of any theoretical system. In the mechanical understanding of the world stemming from scientific materialism, the mind is represented by the machine. In our contemporary perversion, the mind is represented by the electronic computer: the creativity and potentiality of the human mind is reduced to the mechanical and electronic manipulations of the logical and programmed machine. Just as scientific materialism led our culture to reduce the world itself to the image of the machine, so did it lead us to reduce the mind as well to the level of a mechanical device. Ironically, it was mathematical and philosophic work based on the assumption that acts of mind were acts of a machine that finally shattered the assumption of machine-mind altogether. Only in pursuing our convictions of the mind as machine to the bitter inhuman limits did we as a culture break through to a fuller truth.

---

in pursuing our convictions of the mind as machine to the bitter inhuman limits did we as a culture break through to a fuller truth.

Through the work of Kurt Goedel, Alfred North Whitehead, Bertrand Russell, David Hilbert, Gottlob Frege, Guiseppe Peano, Gerrit Manoury, and Luitzen Brouwer we have escaped the confinement of the machine mentality and have transcended the reductionistic world view in its mind-machine paradigm. What is established

14

in formal mathematical proof is the incompleteness of the theoretical system for arriving at the full truth. What has

What is established in formal mathematical proof is the incompleteness of the theoretical system for arriving at the full truth.

been grasped in the clarity of mathematical language is the impossibility of reducing human creativity to the logical process of the machine. For in any mathematical or logical system, the human will eventually arrive at notions that are beyond the power of proof within the system itself.

The understanding of mind in the classical scientific age is that of the electronic computer; the understanding of mind in the emerging era is found in the ineffable depths of the human spirit. For what has been established is that the ground of truth is not and can not be found in the axioms on the page. The judgement of truth is not bound within any system however complex, is not found within any machine, however richly interconnected it might be. The ground of truth and the ground of the creative act

in any mathematical or logical system, the human will eventually arrive at notions that are beyond the power of proof within the system itself.

15

that leaps beyond all theoretical systems is the human spirit. An emerging symbol for the human spirit is a well of creativity from which truth gushes forth and becomes manifest in the creations of the human being.

human spirit is the space wherein the divine truth becomes manifest in the creations of the human being.

The understanding of the emerging era is that the stunning power of creativity of the human being is rooted in the divine plenary emptiness that is inseparably interinvolved with the human spirit. We create the global civilization taking this understanding as our grounding of the human person. We begin with the understanding of the human spirit as interinvolved with the dark plenary creativity of the divine word, and remake our world and our relationships in our world as well as ourselves from this foundation.

The Creation-Centered Spiritual Tradition

The third boiling point is the revisioning of Western religious thought by way of the creation-centered spiritual tradition. This revisioning has been a team process involving many scholars and activists in twentieth century faith life. Some of the persons who have contributed directly or indirectly to this revisioning include Teilhard de Chardin, Nicolas Berdaev, M.D.

16

Chenu, Josef Pieper, Thomas Merton, Edward Schillebeeckx, Martin Luther King, Jr., Claus Westermann, Krister Stendahl, Rosemary Ruether, Gerhard Von Rad, Roland Murphy, Walter Brueggemann, Helen Kenik, Gustavo Gutieriez, Jose Miranda, Jon Sobrino, Thomas Berry. This understanding of creation itself as a divine locus represents the culmination of the greatest creative achievement in critical Biblical scholarship of the past two centuries. It also represents a profound return to our origins in Western faith: the oldest author of the Hebrew Bible, the Yahwist author, was in the creation-centered tradition. So too were the prophets in great measure. So too was Jesus Christ.

The creation-centered spiritual tradition offers an alternative to much of Christian history for it delineates

hellenism and its dualisms regarding body, feeling and spirit is not Jewish or Biblical thinking and that Augustine's dualistic interpretation of Christianity was a distortion of Jesus' spirituality.

the truth that hellenism and its dualisms regarding body, feeling and spirit is not Jewish or Biblical thinking and that Augustine's dualistic interpretation of Christianity was a distortion of Jesus' spirituality. Since vast portions of both Catholic and Protestant churchlife and polity have been constructed on Augustine's dualistic Neoplatonic world view, spirituality in the West must let go of much of Augustine's thought if it is to immerse itself in the profound wellsprings of Biblical spirituality and contribute to creating a global civilization. Specifically, the presumption that original sin is a valid starting point for

17

spiritual living must be let go of; the preoccupation of Augustine with his own introspective guilt must be let go

the presumption that original sin is a valid starting point for spiritual living must be let go of;

of; his confusion of church with kingdom of God needs to be let go of; and his fear of women and the fear of his own sexuality along with the equating of spirituality with flight from passion needs to be let go of; his reduction of the Biblical word justice (justitia) to privatized righteousness needs to be let go of; his anti-semitism needs to be let go of; his ignoring of the cosmos and the cosmic

confusion of church with kingdom of God needs to be let go of;

Christ needs to be let go of. Many of Augustine's philosophical and theological presuppositions continue to haunt western spirituality and many are the Christians who believe in Augustine much more than they do in Jesus Christ. Augustine's dualistic spiritualisms hang like a millstone around the neck of the mystical body of Christ. It is time that persons with faith ask themselves: Do I believe in the Jewish prophets and in Jesus? Or in Augustine?

To believe in Jesus and the Jewish lineage from which he came is to recover a creation-centered spirituality. This spirituality will not present contemplation as the core of spiritual maturity; it will present compassion as the core of spiritual maturity as Jesus did when he declared at the end of his Sermon on the Mount in Luke's Gospel: "Be you compasssionate as your Creator in heaven is compassionate." The tradition calls to persons' minds and imaginations and bodies once again that each member of the human race is an image of God the Creator and that there will be no peace in the human person or among persons until creativity, God's action, flows through us all. This tradition celebrates the awesome and daring News-- news that deserves to be called Good News for it is good and it is news and not boring, rote repetitions--that humans are divine; that we are endowed by the Divinity with divine beauty and dignity, divine life and grace, and divine responsibility.

To believe in our divinity at the same time that we witness daily our brokenness and capacity for the demonic is the reason why Jesus Christ came: To remind us of our origins as images of God, as sons and daughters of God; to remind us of our responsibility to divinize the universe, to be co-creators with the Creator in healing one another

each member of the human race is an image of God the Creator and that there will be no peace in the human person or among persons until creativity, God's action, flows through us all.

and other creatures, in passing on as much beauty as we have received. The Hebrew Scriptures teach that only God is compassionate. Thus, in calling humanity to compassion, religious faith calls humanity to its divinization. This is the Good News that Jesus announces when he declares that "the Kingdom/Queendom of God is at hand." This news challenges us to be responsible for divine history on our planet. This means that in our capacity for

To believe in our divinity at the same time that we witness daily our brokenness and capacity for the demonic is the reason why Jesus Christ came:

imagination and creativity we are to give birth to compassion. If we fail in this effort divine history will come to an end on our planet. Creation spirituality recovers the cosmos in which humanity finds itself utterly interdependent; it also recovers the cosmos within each divinized human being and calls it forth so that this holy microcosm might dance again in the Creator's holy macrocosm and delight might return to the earth.

II.
THE COSMOGENESIS, CREATIVITY, COMPASSION, THE ROOTS of the GLOBAL CIVILIZATION

In the midst of the global cultural chaos stirring all the civilizations of the planet, the old forms of life and culture and the old structure of being and society are being shaken apart so that the new and radically transformed ways of being might emerge. At one time the Earth housed merely a few tender living beings only to discover eventually that these living beings had covered the globe. Later the Earth housed the tiniest number of human beings, only to discover eventually that these

Today the Earth faces a similar moment of transition when the tenderest actualities in our world are growing to structure the very forms of the global civilization.

humans had completely transformed the globe. Today the Earth faces a similar moment of transition when the tenderest actualities in our world are growing to structure the very forms of the global civilization. What are these precious actualities? They are the scientific story of the Cosmogenesis, the human power of Creativity, and human acts of Compassion. These will ground the global civilization.

Cosmogenesis

Everything that exists boasts a fifteen billion year history. Everything that exists contains within itself the entire history of being in our world. The sun, the Earth, the tree in the backyard, one's fingernail, the Elizabethan drama, the mathematical theorem: each existent in the cosmos has a fifteen billion year family history. Each existent has for its first memory that primeval fireball that initiated the entire cosmic drama at the beginning of time. In the future, our orientation toward any existent thing will be that this thing-in-process has been fifteen billion years in the making.

In the future, our orientation toward any existent thing will be that this thing-in-process has been fifteen billion years in the making.

We understand that the cosmogenesis is a fifteen billion year old dance that began with the primeval fireball; that its first epochal moment was its coalescing into the great systems of galaxies; that it erupted into billions of living beings after the careful nurturance of the Earth; that it deepened its creation with the incomparable emergence of the human person and its language; that it extended its creativity into the shamanic tribal era of humanity with its magic and its cults and its rites; that it gathered itself into the focussed and stable formation of the great axial civilizations; that it soared into a frenzy of creativity with the emergence of the scientific-technological era; and that it is now unfolding in a radically new manifestation of the compassionate global civilization. But this is not the whole story.

We need to develop the story beyond the limits of the mechanical world view of scientific materialism. The new story will not overlook the fact that the human person carries within herself the full fifteen billion year history of the cosmos. She is the most profound and startling and amazing creation of the cosmogenesis as a whole. This amazing creation must be seen as <u>most</u>

23

revelatory of the meaning of the entire cosmogenesis in our moment in time. In the diseased world view of scientific materialism we insisted on the reduction to inert material alone and failed to grasp the necessity of

The new story will not overlook the fact that the human person carries within herself the full fifteen billion year history of the cosmos.

expanding beyond this belittlement of the cosmogenesis. Indeed, if the cosmogenesis, in the very best conditions for creativity, showed itself desiring to create the human being at the very end of the fifteen billion year story, then the human being must be profoundly revelatory of the central desire and aim of the cosmogenesis as a whole. To grasp the essence and purpose of the human being is to see into the central meaning and mystery of the cosmos. The old story attempted to explain the most advanced creatures in terms of the most primitive particles. This is equivalent to looking for the ultimate meaning of the cosmos in the first few minutes of a fifteen billion year history, or to expect to find the full meaning of a novel on its first page. The new story insists that the human being is a source of meaning for the cosmogenesis as a whole. As important as the hadronic and leptonic periods are for the meaning of being and life, the fullest creations of the cosmogenesis--humanity itself --need also to be seen as the locus for the meaning of the

As the most intricate and most profound and most dangerous being in creation, the human being can no longer be neglected in our attempts to fathom the meaning of the cosmos itself.

whole. As the most intricate and most profound and most dangerous being in creation, the human being can no longer be neglected in our attempts to fathom the meaning of the cosmos itself. Only in the new story will we grasp the full truth that we are microcosms that reflect and realize the full macrocosm itself.

Our understanding of the cosmogenesis will begin with the conviction that the desire for compassion and justice and the intelligence and the creativity that are so deeply inter woven in the human, are themselves revelatory of the cosmogenetic dance itself. In dark potentiality, com-passion hovers and enfolds the leptons and the hadrons, the photons and the baryons; compassion is intrinsic to the hydrogen atom, the inorganic minerals and all the hydrocarbons involved in the first emergence of a living being. Indeed, in the emerging era we will understand that the human being is far from being the only being

Indeed, in the emerging era we will understand that the human being is far from being the only being capable of compassion.

capable of compassion. The human is that modality of the cosmogenesis where the compassion inherent in the full cosmos finds its incarnation in the works of the world. The human being is that space where the cosmogenesis is able to exhibit the heart of creation, is able to gather all the compassion implicit throughout creation and bring it forth into actual works of creativity.

25

Creativity

In the future global civilization, the power of human creativity will be valued as the greatest resource on the planet. However much we will cherish copper and oil and coal and soil and water and air and minerals, the greatest resource on the planet will be the human beings well of creative power. Just as today entire nations are governed and guided by concerns for oil, so too in the future the entire civilization will be structured and guided by the valuing, developing, cherishing and deepening of human creativity. Whereas today we devote enormous human energy to extracting the coal and oil from the Earth, in the future we will devote even more energy for extracting--evoking, nurturing, exciting, channeling, transforming--the creative energy of the human person.

Our civilization will devote itself to the nurturance of the creative well of power within the human person because of its understanding that the cosmogenesis is nowhere more powerfully active than in the creative acts of the human person. At the very ground of the human person there is no material, no machine, no disembodied soul, but

The very foundation of the human being is a nothingness, an empty generative potentiality, the divine logos or dabar from which all things of the cosmogenesis spring forth.

rather the empty infinity of plenary potentiality. The very foundation of the human being is a nothingness, an empty generative potentiality, the divine logos or dabar from which all things of the cosmogenesis spring forth. Not only is the human being created out of this nothingness; the living presence of the Godhead springs from this empty nothingness. The full manifestation of the cosmogenesis springs from this fecund and empty fullness. We will devote ourselves to the nurturance of human beings and the creative possibilities inherent in each human being for we will understand that in so doing we are evoking the most fundamental processes of the cosmogenesis as a whole.

In our nurturing of the creativity of the human person, we will reverence all the creations of the human spirit throughout the globe and throughout history. In our work to create the global civilization, we will be guided by the humility of understanding deeply that no one context can contain the fullness of the truth: that no system of thought or language is capable of encompassing all the

---

The North American continent is a most powerful locus of the creative power needed for re-recreating the world.

---

beauty and all the truth and all the goodness of the divine possibilities. And in this respect, Americans have a special responsibility in the creation of the global civilization itself. For in America there are diverse strands from the powerful human creations of our history: there are the scientific and artistic worlds that strongly extend and deepen the intuitions of the Greek axial civilization: there is the spectrum of religions, and the deep religious fervor and passion that we have been given by the great axial Hebrew civilization. There is the unique geographic situation where America touches the edge of both East and West. And even more, there is the great untouched resource of our continent's spiritual treasures: the form of life and being that is the Native American's. The North American continent is a most powerful locus of the creative power needed for re-recreating the world.

COMPASSION: The Meaning of Divinizing Creation

To divinize creation means to return compassion to the cosmos and all earthly beings, ourselves included. And it means to derive compassion from the cosmos by the reverence we show all earthly beings by respecting them, learning from them, listening to them and interacting with them. But the dualisms of western thought have in fact destroyed the very meaning of the word compassion and so we must critique the meaning behind our vocation to divinize creation.

Compassion in spiritual traditions is about three energies. First, compassion means a consciousness or world view of interdependence and interconnections. Compassionate awareness is about the relativity, that is the inter-relationship, of all beings, all time, all space. Thomas

Compassionate awareness is about the relativity, that is the inter-relationship, of all beings, all time, all space.

Merton defined compassion in the following way in a talk he gave hours before he died. "Compassion is a keen awareness of the interdependence of all living things which are all involved in one another and are all part of one another." Compassionate thinking cuts through all dualisms and all separatisms to the ultimate truth that all is interinvolved.

Secondly, compassion means action, action that grows out of the truth of awareness of interconnections and interdependence. The actions we take to heal, to make whole, to bring together, to mend--all these are actions of compassion for they are actions of removing obstacles to interdependence and one-ing. The greatest single obstacle to compassion in human history has been and still is: Injustice. Injustice represents the triumph of power-over and power-under activity which is always a sado-

---

compassion means action, action that grows out of the truth of awareness of interconnections and interdependence.

---

masochistic activity. Injustice remains the greatest single obstacle to healing persons and animals and all creatures. For that reason our work at undoing injustices and creating movements and alternative organizations of justice and our work in imaginatively protesting injustice is all compassionate action.

Thirdly, compassion is about celebration. People who cannot celebrate do not yet know what compassion is. For compassion is about passion-with (from the latin <u>cum</u>

29

patior) and celebration is the letting go that takes place when we truly feel with. Celebration does not take place when we feel over or superior (there lies passion over or sadism); nor if we feel under or inferior (there lies passion under or masochism); nor if we must be in control. Compassion requires equality in our feelings toward self and

People who cannot celebrate do not yet know what compassion is.

others including all creatures, not just human ones. Because compassion is a kind of passion, it is a way of life or spirituality which is at home with deep feelings whether of anger and moral outrage or of desire. The gift of compassion is the gift of directing, channeling, disciplining these feelings toward directions of healing and making one. In our culture the art of celebration and of savoring is itself a profound way of healing for in a

the art of celebration and of savoring is itself a profound way of healing

culture as compulsively materialistic and consumer-oriented as ours the art of celebration is largely lost.

The boiling point cited above from microphysics finds its counterpart in today's religious movements. This ought to be no surprise to any believer since all grace builds on nature and all theology builds on our views of nature. As those views alter, so do our theologies. The boiling point that we have called the indivisibility of the quantum finds

> *The mystery of the Incarnation itself calls each of us to be a child of God and a birther of God.*

its spiritual expression in Compassion, an awareness that no creature is separate from any other and no joy and no pain are apart from one's own. Compassion also finds a spiritual expression in the breakdown of the dualism between God and humanity. The mystery of the Incarnation itself calls each of us to be a child of God and a birther of God. God is no longer an object, not even the greatest or most awesome object, in the universe. God's history and humanity's are inseparable. This same theme finds a profound spiritual expression as well in the preaching of Jesus Christ that the "Kingdom/Queendom of God is at hand." This sense of realized eschatology, of the future being already among us, initiates a break-through in time and space that brings hope to the hearts and hands of people of good will everywhere. It also brings awesome responsibility, for our life's work is to contribute to the fleshing out and the incarnation of this Good News. The creation tradition is a tradition of God-with-Us, of Emmanuel. Not of God-over-us or God-

> *This spirituality of blessing announces a way of life in which joy and delight are passed to one another in the midst of our darkness and our deep experiences of nothingness.*

judging-us. This spirituality of blessing announces a way

31

of life in which joy and delight are passed to one another in the midst of our darkness and our deep experiences of nothingness. Hope feeds those who struggle for justice sake.

Thus today's physics supports a central theme of the creation-centered spiritual tradition of the West: Interdependence and wholeness and compassion by way of justice, love and celebration of our common existence.

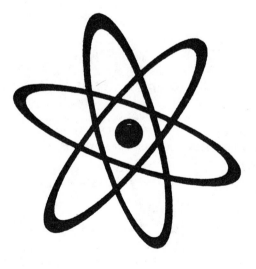

III.

REVISIONING SCIENCE, RELIGION and THE ART OF LIVING

In a new and global civilization divinized by an awareness of cosmogenesis, creativity and compassion, a passion for recreating culture will erupt everywhere. In particular we foresee that this boiling over will permeate the areas of science, religion and the art of living.

Science

Science and mathematics are in their infancy. If we are to insure that they continue to create and enable humans to transform the world as a whole, their core of mysticism must be celebrated. A mystical core of activity is the existential reality of every creative scientist. By mysticism here we mean that deep mystery of being swept into the heart of thinking and searching and imagining and creating that is every scientist's in the thrall of the work. The great and central mystery of being seized by the throbbing and unfathomable allurement itself, being seized up and carried on currents of being that run in the heart of the cosmogenesis itself. By mysticism we mean that deep feeling of the scientist of

> *By mysticism here we mean that deep mystery of being swept into the heart of thinking and searching and imagining and creating that is every scientist's in the thrall of the work.*

having been gathered into a movement of being that is morphogenetically homologous with the surging energy in the stars.

The existential actuality of the creativity of the scientist must be explicitly articulated in the culture so that the great zest for the scientific enterprise will be celebrated and deepened. Without this celebration scientific culture becomes machine-like. Creativity dies. A science-technology based on the machine will surely lead to killing the zest for the scientific enterprise. It is difficult to imagine that the sciences could lapse into triviality, and yet this happened once before in western history when

A science-technology based on the machine will surely lead to killing the zest for the scientific enterprise.

Augustine's repudiation of the scientific mind contributed to science's vanishing from European civilization for over a thousand years. As Albert Einstein said: "the most important function of art and science is to awaken the cosmic religious feeling and keep it alive."

When the mystery of creativity is celebrated in our culture we will see scientists and mathematicians profoundly encouraged to transcend the boundaries of the scientific enterprise as it now exists. Without the celebration of the mystery and mysticism of human

Without the celebration of the mystery and mysticism of human creativity, we sink into a machine mentality, and the inevitable deadening of human imagination.

creativity, we sink into a machine mentality, and the inevitable deadening of human imagination.

But as crucial as the need for the celebration of the mysticism of science might be, it does not compare with the enormous need for a prophetic revisioning of science. What we propose is a radical reversal of thought that dwarfs the Copernican reversal. We must transform our

We must go beyond and beneath the arrogant position of the isolated and separated human knower of nature, creation as a whole,

thinking until we know that it is the cosmogenesis that has nurtured our creating of science. We must go beyond and beneath the arrogant position of the isolated and separated human knower of nature. We must revision science with the beginning point of the cosmogenesis: the cosmos as a whole has developed us and taught us and nurtured us, and our creation of science is itself from the compassion of the cosmogenesis as a totality.

We must learn to regard ourselves as that permeable space wherein science itself could come into existence within the cosmos. The cosmogenesis would be unable to express the actualities of science without the human; and the human would be unable to create the scientific theories without the patient teaching of the cosmogenesis. We provide the cosmos with a space where the powerful process of nature is grasped in language in order to deepen and broaden the works of justice and transformation. The central questions we put to all the theories of science and the creations of technology must be these: What possibilities for love-justice has the cosmogenesis suddenly been given? What acts of justice are now possible within the cosmogenesis as a whole? What acts of love and what acts of compassion are suddenly possible, now that the cosmogenesis has carefully nurtured our creativity and our creation of this science and this technology? Without posing these

---

What acts of love and what acts of compassion are suddenly possible, now that the cosmogenesis has carefully nurtured our creativity and our creation of this science and this technology?

---

questions to themselves scientists and technologists will continue to enable military industrial Nation-states to play havoc with the planet.

The revisioning of science in a broad manner will be based on the celebration of the mystical core of energetic interest in the creative activities of the scientist; and upon the growth in maturity of humanity as a whole as we learn to understand science-technology as the cosmogenesis's work through the human for the purpose of justice, love, compassion.

Religion

There will be no era of a global civilization without global religions intermixing in profound dialogue and interpenetration. And this cannot happen until religions let go of

37

themselves as religions and recover themselves as spiritualities or ways of life. When this happens, then true global religious ecumenism will erupt and bless this planet. Essential to the recovery of religion as spirituality in the West is a mystical awakening and appreciation of its own earth-bound and creation-centered mystics. A critical study of such faith-lovers as Hildegarde of Bingen, Francis of Assisi, Thomas Aquinas, Mechtild of Magdeburg, Meister Eckhart, Julian of Norwich, Nicholas of Cusa, John of the Cross, to name a few, will reveal that the cosmos has not always been exiled in Western faith practice.

religions must let go of themselves as religions and recover themselves as spiritualities or ways of life.

The study and living of such western mystics by westerners also opens the door to deep spiritual ecumenism with other traditions. Native American spirituality, for example, is readily understood by a true follower of Saint Francis of Assisi or Julian of Norwich and Mechtild of Magdeburg who drew heavily as did Meister Eckhart from the chthonic and matriarchal religious period of human history. Buddhists and Hindus already lay claims to shared insights and practice with Meister Eckhart who, ironically, is the most Jewish and Biblical spiritual writer in 1900 years of Christian history. Yes, it is at the level of the mystics, healthily chosen and understood, that the true ecumenical dialogue waits to happen.

When faith in the West moves from Fall/Redemption suppositions wherein sin is the first and often last topic dwelt on to the creation-centered tradition wherein existence and life as a gift are celebrated and passed on, tremendous opportunities for a renewal of ritual and worship arise. The return of cosmic consciousness; of the

---

When faith in the West moves from Fall/Redemption suppositions wherein sin is the first and often last topic dwelt on to the creation centered tradition wherein existence and life as a gift are celebrated and passed on, tremendous opportunities for a renewal of ritual and worship arise.

---

dark; of silence; of mystery; of depth; of the non verbal; of the curved is promised. Meditation will be recovered in our churches and our daily lives--but not merely meditation on given symbols or objects but meditation as a form of centering by giving birth; in other words, art as meditation.

In this regard an ecumenical era is eager to be born between art and spirituality. This does not mean that artists must choose a so-called religious object as a subject for art (for in an interdependent universe there

---

art is to be understood as an expression of the deepest and therefore most communal dimension of humanity on the one hand; and that religious faith is meant to be the same.

---

are no objects) but rather that art is to be understood as an expression of the deepest and therefore most communal dimension of humanity on the one hand; and that religous faith is meant to be the same. In fact, a critical spirituality will readily grasp the truth of the matter that it is the artists of western culture the past few centuries who have kept burning the spark of humanity's divinization often with whiter heat than have many a canonized saint. Mozart, Bach, Mahler, Beethoven, Goethe, Novalis, Chagall, Dickens, Dickenson, Rilke, have among countless others been ecumenists of art and spirituality. It is time a breakthrough occurred and a new ecumenism began at grass root levels among artists and believers. No greater proof of this is needed than the sad and sorry state of church music and liturgy today wherein sentimental music and lyrics trivialize worship and bore what few worshippers still come to such liturgical events.

Religion must continue its movement from preoccupation with salvation as righteousness to preaching and living salvation as justice-making. Great strides have been made in this regard even in the past twenty years--the bishops of the Roman Catholic church in their Synod in Rome put it well when they said that "social justice is a

---

Religion must continue its movement from preoccupation with salvation as righteousness to preaching and living salvation as justice-making.

---

constitutive element of the Gospel." But there can be no justice in a world of interdependence without global consciousness and so at this level too churches and

40

synogogues and other bodies of spiritual tradition must awaken people to the suffering and pain that too parochial a view of politics or economic or art or worship inculcate. Religion itself must become more and more self-critical. For what kind of witness is it to preach justice to that continent or this country when injustice in the form of oppression of women, for example, calls from one's own religious back yard? The justice demanded of a compassionate religious faith requires that women be welcomed with their talents and gifts into a role of equality in spiritual dialogue and celebration. Indeed,

many of the most healing and hope-filled rituals of our time are being led by women of deep faith and enduring hope.

many of the most healing and hope-filled rituals of our time are being created and led by women of deep faith and enduring hope.

In the future religion will be nurtured by deep meditation and entry into the meaning of humanity as the image of God. In this spiritual vision the discipline of creativity will be more important than obedience. Or, to put it another way, religious obedience will be expressed in obedience to the creative impulse and the image of God or imagination. Spiritual imagination will find a local and microcosmic expression in a renewed liturgy, one that is born from the earth and from persons close to the earth. Its eschatological and unmistakable sign will be celebration. The cosmos celebrated; joy and hope anticipated. Like the cosmos it will be circular or Sara Circle in its dynamic and not linear. It will announce the future by practicing it. The practice of justice and compassion are always ahead of their time and never welcomed as timely by those in power.

---

religious obedience will be expressed in obedience to the creative impulse and the image of God or imagination.

In short, renewed religious faith will be universal and global in the full sense while it retains local roots at the level of practice in justice-making and celebration and at the level of support offered to fellow journeyers.

The second boiling point in contemporary culture, this one derived from mathematics, we have called the essential incompleteness of any theoretical system. This truth has found its religious expression in our time in the ecumenical movement. It challenges all believers to recognize the difference between spirituality or a way of life and the claims of religion. No religion is complete in itself. And no spiritual tradition can ignore the diverse and beautiful ways in which God has become incarnate in other cultures, other human periods and other spiritual traditions. This truth requires an ecclesial and institutional humility which can be understood as a

---

no spiritual tradition can ignore the diverse and beautiful ways in which God has become incarnate in other cultures, other human periods and other spiritual traditions.

---

theological recognition of the difference between church and Kingdom/Queendom of God. For while the Good News is that the Kingdom/Queendom of God has begun, the bad news is that it has not fully begun and is never fully incarnated--much less institutionalized--in any one form or expression of spirituality. The Holy Spirit will

The Holy Spirit will not be locked in to any one form of religious faith.

not be locked in to any one form of religious faith.

We People of God--all the People of creation--need one another and all the wisdom we can derive from one another. Global interdependence requires a global ecumenical awakening so that the power and blessing of healing and compassion that all faiths can teach their people might ignite all peoples of the world in which we live. The ecumenical movement - understood as the energizing of all faiths of this planet by celebration, by interaction for justice and compassion, by dialogue and mutual study of one another's faiths - holds out for the human race one of its last great hopes for redemption.

articulating of the essential incompleteness of any theoretical system of any kind including a religious one might hasten a fuller and more grass roots expression of this movement.

While much has been accomplished in our century and in particular among Western religious traditions in the way of shared activity and mutual study and appreciation, still the articulating of the essential incompleteness of any theoretical system of any kind including a religious one might hasten a fuller and more grass roots expression of this movement.

But the religion of the future will be ecumenical not only in the religious sense of dialogue with religious traditions. Spiritual traditions need to dialogue with artists, feminists, scientists. Other professionals too must enter this ecumenical dialogue: The work of doctors and lawyers, of economists and politicians, media workers and manual workers, will be work in dialogue with their own spiritual values and traditions as human beings and citizens

religious faith will not seek its own perpetuation but will believe deeply enough that it can let go of its own privileged positions in order to be among the least and the poorest.

responsible to the global village. A renewed spirituality will allow this dialogue to happen for such a religious faith will not seek its own perpetuation but will believe deeply enough that it can let go of its own privileged positions in order to be among the least and the poorest. In other words, faith must have faith in itself and this of an unselfconscious kind. Only then is it free to be transparent and thus truly intermingle like leaven does in dough in a profoundly ecumenical way with all energies of human civilization. It is lack of faith and fear of death and mortality that has so often forced religion into quests

44

for immortality expressed by the compulsion for bigger buildings or other forms of power-as-clinging. While structures will always be necessary for religious faith, no one structure and no one way of practice is ever complete. Until religion itself can learn to let go, how can people receive the instruction that Letting Go is a deep and essential part of the spiritual journey for us all?

Religion must start believing once again and quit feeling sorry for itself.

Religion must start believing once again and quit feeling sorry for itself vis a'vis a so-called "secular world" or "atheistic world" or "scientific world" or "world of artists." Otherwise it will have no leaven to offer humankind and humankind will be the losers.

The Art of Living:
Learning, Working, Being

A civilization that understands itself as a community dedicated to creating the beautiful will begin to reverence life more. The reverencing of life and this

The reverencing of life and this passing on of reverence and the disciplines for reverencing life constitutes the heart of all human learning.

passing on of reverence and the disciplines for reverencing life constitutes the heart of all human learning. The new global civilization requires that we awaken ourselves and our educational institutions of all kinds to the priority of aesthetic consciousness. Aesthetic feeling is not emotion: rather, aesthetic feeling grounds all being and creating of the human.

Aesthetic feeling is not emotion: rather, aesthetic feeling grounds all being and creating of the human.

Because recent educational practice is so deeply cemented into a conceptual mode of education, it is necessary to elaborate somewhat on these comments. Knowledge of a conceptual kind is a light of the highest value in education. The darkness of superstition will engulf any civilization that is not committed to established and powerful forms of conceptual knowledge. Aesthetic feeling, on the other hand, has been exiled from western education for centuries. To return aesthetic feeling to our educational forms means to structure into our future education the teaching of the experiential, the prelogical, and process awareness--all forms of knowing

the role of art as a centering or meditation process for all persons is absolutely essential.

that are central to the act of creativity. Our western education has been overconcerned with knowledge and has failed to stress the creating of knowledge. We need to

46

penetrate ever more deeply into the theory and practice of creating knowledge in a time of cultural transformation like ours. Here the role of art as a centering or meditation process for all persons is absolutely essential.

Education and learning itself have too often been understood to be a preparation for adult life. This leaves one with the impression that adults have all the answers and can cease learning. Then manipulation of what is, substitutes for the art of living. This way lies the death of adult spiritual growth. This way lies ennui and boredom, lack of excitement at living, and ultimately violence and frustration among the young who see no living in depth from adults. In this way a culture is arrested at an adolescent level of entertainment, sexuality, ego-consciousness. Passion for living and the sharing of life loses its rightful place in people's hearts

with the loss of passion there follows the exile of compassion.

and with the loss of passion there follows the exile of compassion.

The new art of living requires an awareness that learning constitutes the very process of the life of a human being and that when learning stops a person stops and a civilization dies. Learning is a process that has no end as long as one is in this world. The world itself is the primary school for learning and needs to be understood as that. Learning constitutes the deepest prayer of the human person, the deepest awareness that she or he is a modality of process reflecting the cosmogenesis as a

47

whole, a microcosm in a beautiful macrocosm.

Learning constitutes the deepest prayer of the human person, the deepest awareness that she or he is a modality of process reflecting the cosmogenesis as a whole, a microcosm in a beautiful macrocosm.

The art of living as the art of learning spills over into work and work spills over into learning. Work is where most adults spend their time, their energy, their efforts, their talent. All work is spiritual work when it contributes to the on-going transformation of cosmos by way of the new civilization. All work is demonic which saps energy from this movement to wholeness. The greatest crime people perpetrate on other people is excluding them from good work. Unemployment is a root cause of violence world-wide in our time. Still, by tapping human creativity we can put people to good work and restructure our meanings or work.

All work is spiritual work when it contributes to the on-going transformation of cosmos by way of the new civilization. All work is demonic which saps energy from this movement to wholeness.

But to be true to work and the depth of its task we need always to make clear that the greatest thing to come out of the factory is the factory worker; the greatest thing to emerge from the mine is the miner; the greatest thing to come out of the farm is the farmer. To miss this essential value is to confuse means with ends and to make idols of our work. Work is healthiest when it blends with art or self-expression. And when both art and work become indistinguishable from play, then humanity has indeed tasted its best and most divine fruitfulness.

At the level of play all life becomes being, and being and life become one cause for celebration. A life without

> *A life without awareness of being is not a human life; it is an insult to the cosmos and the fifteen-billion-year effort by the cosmos to birth humanity.*

awareness of being is not a human life; it is an insult to the cosmos and the fifteen-billion-year effort by the cosmos to birth humanity. By being we mean existence, that which all creation has in common. Humanity cannot live in a sense of peace with itself or with others when an experience of being is not developed and nurtured. It is being itself that is the most precious of all gifts and the most divine. It is being that we celebrate most radically when we truly let go and celebrate.

But to live, learn and work at the level of the art of being requires a constant simplifying of our lives; a constant letting go; a willingness to be alone-with-being and not cover being up with noisiness, business, brick-bracks, and compulsions to clinging. Consumerism and being are incompatible. Human beings are not on earth to manufacture consumer items for one another but to share being; to celebrate being; to reverence being; and to fall ever more deeply in love and thankfulness for being. To birth being is the awesome gift of being a parent in either a literal or a symbolic sense; the truth of it is learned when one buries one's parents and realizes the preciousness of one's own being-on-earth. The great western mystic Meister Eckhart declared that "being is God" and if we understood this we would understand how divine our

---

Human beings are not on earth to manufacture consumer items for one another but to share being; to celebrate being; to reverence being; and to fall ever more deeply in love and thankfulness for being.

---

lives already are. And how much simple delight there is to share when injustice is let go of and compassion and beauty are shared. In letting go we return to our origins, our well-springs of energy, even to nothingness. Out of this emptiness new creation can emerge.

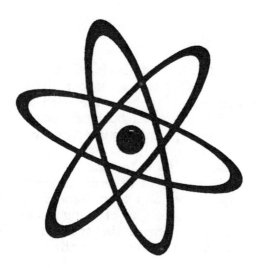

EPILOGUE

An Invitation To
A Beautiful Adventure

We have defined civilization as a community's quest to create the beautiful and we have outlined what the beauty is that the human race needs to survive today. The community at stake is not a lonely tribe or a faltering nation. It is the entire race called human. It is the global village community we speak of. The beauty alluring us all is the beauty of cosmogenesis which by its vastness, its patience in awaiting us for fifteen billion years, its mysterious harmony and delightfulness is simply beautiful and a mirror of our microcosmic beauty. The opposite of cosmogenesis--privitization of people and their thinking, of science or religion or both, is very simply put, ugly. And it leads to the ugliness of raw greed, naked competition, boredom and the triumph of ego-power at the expense of compassion. Compassion with its energies of interdependence, justice and celebration is always beautiful. And its opposite--apathy, self-satisfaction, indifference to the pain and pleasure of others--is ugly.

Justice-making is always beauty and the refusal to participate in celebrating existence is always ugly and creates ugliness such as luxury living in the midst of human squalor, decadent pleasure-seeking in the midst of humans in need of basics.

Justice-making is always beautiful and the refusal to participate in celebrating existence is always ugly and creates ugliness such as luxury living in the midst of human squalor, decadent pleasure-seeking in the midst of humans in need of basics. Ecumenism is beautiful. Its opposite, rabid prostelytizing born of parochial self-justification and refusal to learn from other spiritual traditions is always ugly and leads to war and the cutting off of heart-to-heart and mind-to-mind exchange. The refusal to create learning together is always ugly.

To recover the cosmos both within us and around us, and moreover to be agents or co-creators in re-creating this cosmos--this is a beautiful adventure. Today everyone on our planet is invited to this festival of being and creating. The only ticket required for entry is a willingness to let go, and a courageous faith in our potential to create beauty anew.

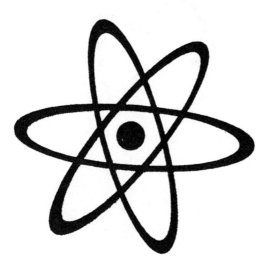

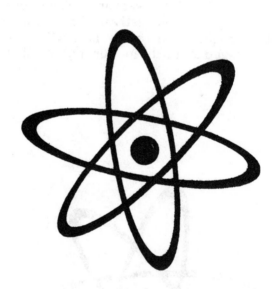

NOTES